While every precaution has been taken in the prepa
publisher assumes no responsibility for errors or on
resulting from the use of the information containec

THE LOW-FAT LIFESTYLE: TIPS AND RECIPES FOR A
HEALTHIER HEART

First edition. March 18, 2024.

ISBN: 979-8224726080

Written by Boughton Richard Aubrey.

Table of Contents

The Low-Fat Lifestyle: Tips and Recipes for a Healthier Heart

Carrot and ginger soup

Ingredients:

- 8 medium carrots
- 1 small onion
- 2 cloves of garlic
- 1 inch piece of ginger
- 4 cups of vegetable broth
- Salt and pepper to taste

Equipment:

1. Pot
2. Wooden spoon
3. Knife
4. Blender
5. Ladle

Methods:

Step 1: Peel and chop 1 pound of carrots and 1 onion.

Step 2: Heat 2 tablespoons of olive oil in a large pot over medium heat.

Step 3: Add the chopped carrots and onion to the pot and cook until softened, about 5 minutes.

Step 4: Add 2 cloves of minced garlic and 1 tablespoon of grated ginger to the pot and cook for another 1-2 minutes.

Step 5: Pour in 4 cups of vegetable broth and bring to a simmer.

Step 6: Once simmering, reduce heat and let the soup cook for 20-25 minutes.

Step 7: Use an immersion blender to blend the soup until smooth.

Step 8: Season with salt and pepper to taste before serving.

Helpful Tips:

1. Start by sautéing onions and minced ginger in olive oil for extra flavor.
2. Use fresh carrots that are sweet and tender for the best taste.
3. Add vegetable broth and simmer until the carrots are soft.
4. Blend the soup until smooth for a creamy texture.

5. For a touch of sweetness, add a splash of maple syrup or honey.

6. Finish with a garnish of fresh chopped parsley or a dollop of Greek yogurt.

7. Serve hot with a side of crusty bread or a light salad.

8. Refrigerate any leftovers in an airtight container for up to 4 days.

Coconut crusted shrimp with mango salsa

Ingredients:
- 1 lb shrimp
- 1 cup shredded coconut
- 1/2 cup flour
- 1 egg
- 1 mango
- 1/2 red onion
- 1 jalapeno
- 1 lime
- salt and pepper

Equipment:
1. Cutting board
2. Knife
3. Frying pan
4. Mixing bowl
5. Tongs

Methods:
Step 1: Preheat the oven to 400°F and line a baking sheet with parchment paper.

Step 2: Peel and devein shrimp, leaving tails on.

Step 3: In one bowl, mix shredded coconut, breadcrumbs, and seasonings.

Step 4: In another bowl, whisk egg whites until frothy.

Step 5: Dip each shrimp in egg whites, then coat with coconut mixture.

Step 6: Place coated shrimp on the baking sheet.

Step 7: Bake for 10-12 minutes, or until shrimp is pink and coconut is golden brown.

Step 8: While shrimp is baking, prepare mango salsa by mixing diced mango, red onion, cilantro, lime juice, and salt.

Step 9: Serve cooked shrimp with mango salsa on top. Enjoy!

Helpful Tips:

1. Make sure to devein and remove the shells from the shrimp before coating with coconut.

2. Use fresh coconut flakes for a more vibrant flavor and texture.

3. Season the shrimp with salt, pepper, and a touch of cayenne pepper for added spice.

4. Press the coconut onto the shrimp firmly to ensure it sticks well and forms a crispy crust.

5. Serve the coconut crusted shrimp with a tangy mango salsa for a refreshing contrast of flavors.

6. Garnish with fresh cilantro or lime wedges for a burst of freshness.

Lemon garlic marinated chicken thighs

Ingredients:

- 8 boneless, skinless chicken thighs
- 1/4 cup olive oil
- 1/4 cup lemon juice
- 4 cloves garlic, minced
- 1 tsp salt
- 1/2 tsp black pepper

Equipment:

1. Mixing bowl
2. Whisk
3. Grill pan
4. Tongs
5. Basting brush

Methods:

Step 1: In a small bowl, combine lemon juice, minced garlic, olive oil, salt, pepper, and chopped fresh herbs.

Step 2: Place chicken thighs in a resealable plastic bag and pour the marinade over them.

Step 3: Seal the bag and massage the marinade into the chicken, ensuring each piece is coated.

Step 4: Marinate in the refrigerator for at least 30 minutes, up to overnight.

Step 5: Preheat grill to medium-high heat.

Step 6: Remove chicken from the marinade and discard excess.

Step 7: Grill chicken thighs for 6-8 minutes per side, until fully cooked.

Step 8: Serve and enjoy!

Helpful Tips:

1. In a large bowl, mix together lemon juice, minced garlic, olive oil, salt, pepper, and any other desired seasonings.

2. Add chicken thighs to the marinade, ensuring they are fully coated, and let them marinate in the fridge for at least 30 minutes (overnight for best results).

3. Preheat a grill or skillet over medium-high heat and cook the chicken thighs for 6-8 minutes per side, or until they reach an internal temperature of 165°F.

4. Let the chicken rest for a few minutes before serving to retain juices and tenderness.

5. Garnish with fresh herbs or a squeeze of lemon before serving. Enjoy!

Green bean and cherry tomato salad with balsamic vinaigrette

Ingredients:
- 1 pound green beans
- 1 cup cherry tomatoes
- 1/4 cup balsamic vinegar
- 2 tablespoons olive oil

Equipment:
1. Mixing bowl
2. Whisk
3. Salad tongs
4. Serving platter
5. Measuring spoons

Methods:
Step 1: Wash and trim the green beans.

Step 2: Boil a pot of water and blanch the green beans for 2-3 minutes.

Step 3: Prepare a bowl of ice water and immediately transfer the green beans into it to stop the cooking process.

Step 4: Cut the cherry tomatoes in half and add them to a large salad bowl.

Step 5: Drain the green beans and add them to the salad bowl with the cherry tomatoes.

Step 6: In a small bowl, whisk together balsamic vinegar, olive oil, Dijon mustard, salt, and pepper to make the vinaigrette.

Step 7: Pour the dressing over the salad and toss to combine.

Step 8: Serve and enjoy!

Helpful Tips:
1. Start by blanching the green beans in boiling water for a few minutes until they are bright green and slightly tender.

2. Shock the green beans in ice water to stop the cooking process and maintain their vibrant color.

3. Slice the cherry tomatoes in half to release their juices and flavors.

4. Make a simple balsamic vinaigrette by combining balsamic vinegar, olive oil, Dijon mustard, honey, salt, and pepper in a jar and shaking vigorously.

5. Toss the blanched green beans and cherry tomatoes with the balsamic vinaigrette just before serving to ensure the salad stays crisp and fresh.

Roasted beet and arugula salad with goat cheese

Ingredients:
- 4 medium beets
- 4 cups arugula
- 1/2 cup crumbled goat cheese
- 1/4 cup olive oil
- Salt and pepper to taste

Equipment:
1. Mixing bowl
2. Salad tongs
3. Grater
4. Baking sheet
5. Salad spinner

Methods:
Step 1: Preheat the oven to 400°F and line a baking sheet with foil.

Step 2: Wash and peel 3 medium beets, then chop into 1-inch cubes.

Step 3: Toss the beet cubes with olive oil, salt, and pepper on the baking sheet.

Step 4: Roast the beets in the oven for 30-35 minutes, or until they are tender.

Step 5: In a large bowl, toss arugula with balsamic vinaigrette.

Step 6: Arrange the roasted beets on top of the arugula.

Step 7: Crumble goat cheese over the salad.

Step 8: Serve immediately and enjoy your roasted beet and arugula salad with goat cheese!

Helpful Tips:
1. Preheat your oven to 400°F (200°C) and line a baking sheet with parchment paper.

2. Wash and peel your beets, then slice them into thin rounds or cubes.

3. Toss the beet slices with olive oil, salt, and pepper before placing them on the baking sheet in a single layer.

4. Roast the beets for about 25-30 minutes, or until they are tender and caramelized.

5. While the beets are roasting, assemble your salad by tossing arugula with a simple vinaigrette dressing.

6. Once the beets are done, allow them to cool slightly before adding them to the salad.

7. Finally, crumble some goat cheese on top of the salad for a creamy and tangy finish. Enjoy your delicious and nutritious roasted beet and arugula salad!

Baked cod with lemon caper sauce

Ingredients:
- 4 pieces of cod fillet
- 1/2 cup of lemon juice
- 2 tablespoons of capers
- 2 cloves of garlic
- Salt and pepper to taste

Equipment:
1. Baking dish
2. Whisk
3. Saucepan
4. Knife
5. Cutting board

Methods:
Step 1: Preheat the oven to 400°F.

Step 2: Season the cod fillets with salt and pepper.

Step 3: Place the fillets in a baking dish.

Step 4: In a small bowl, mix together lemon juice, capers, garlic, and olive oil.

Step 5: Pour the sauce over the cod fillets.

Step 6: Cover the baking dish with foil and bake for 15-20 minutes, or until the fish is opaque and flakes easily with a fork.

Step 7: Remove the foil and broil for an additional 3-5 minutes to lightly brown the top.

Step 8: Serve the baked cod with lemon caper sauce hot and enjoy!

Helpful Tips:
1. Preheat your oven to 375°F and lightly grease a baking dish.

2. Season the cod fillets with salt and pepper before placing them in the baking dish.

3. In a small saucepan, combine lemon juice, capers, butter, and garlic over low heat until the butter is melted.

4. Pour the lemon caper sauce over the cod fillets.

5. Bake in the preheated oven for 15-20 minutes, or until the fish flakes easily with a fork.

6. Serve the baked cod with a side of steamed vegetables or a salad for a complete meal. Enjoy!

Spaghetti squash with turkey meatballs and marinara sauce

Ingredients:
- 1 medium spaghetti squash
- 1 lb ground turkey
- 1 cup marinara sauce
- 1/4 cup bread crumbs

Equipment:
1. Cutting board
2. Knife
3. Mixing bowl
4. Skillet
5. Baking sheet

Methods:
Step 1: Preheat the oven to 400°F.

Step 2: Cut the spaghetti squash in half lengthwise and remove the seeds.

Step 3: Place the squash halves on a baking sheet, cut side down, and roast for 45-50 minutes, or until the flesh is tender.

Step 4: While the squash is roasting, prepare the turkey meatballs by mixing ground turkey, breadcrumbs, Parmesan cheese, egg, and seasonings in a bowl. Form into meatballs and bake in the oven for 20-25 minutes.

Step 5: Heat up marinara sauce in a saucepan on the stove.

Step 6: Once the squash and meatballs are done, use a fork to scrape the squash flesh into strands.

Step 7: Serve the spaghetti squash topped with turkey meatballs and marinara sauce. Enjoy!

Helpful Tips:
1. Preheat oven to 400°F.

2. Cut spaghetti squash in half lengthwise, scoop out seeds, and place face down on baking sheet with a little water. Bake for 40-50 minutes until tender.

3. Mix ground turkey with breadcrumbs, Parmesan cheese, Italian seasoning, garlic powder, salt, and pepper. Form into meatballs and bake for 20-25 minutes.

4. Heat marinara sauce in a saucepan.

5. Use a fork to scrape the cooked spaghetti squash into "noodles."

6. Serve turkey meatballs on top of spaghetti squash noodles with marinara sauce. Enjoy!

Chicken and vegetable stir-fry with teriyaki sauce

Ingredients:
- 1 lb boneless, skinless chicken breast
- 1 cup of broccoli florets
- 1 red bell pepper, sliced
- 1/2 cup teriyaki sauce

Equipment:
1. Wok
2. Cooking spoon
3. Knife
4. Cutting board
5. Measuring cups
6. Tongs

Methods:
Step 1: Marinate thinly sliced chicken breast in teriyaki sauce for 30 minutes.

Step 2: Heat oil in a large skillet or wok over medium-high heat.

Step 3: Add the marinated chicken and cook until browned and cooked through.

Step 4: Remove chicken from skillet and set aside.

Step 5: Add sliced bell peppers, broccoli, and snap peas to the skillet.

Step 6: Stir-fry the vegetables until they are tender-crisp.

Step 7: Return the chicken to the skillet and pour in the remaining teriyaki sauce.

Step 8: Cook for an additional 2-3 minutes, stirring constantly.

Step 9: Serve hot over cooked rice. Enjoy your delicious chicken and vegetable stir-fry!

Helpful Tips:
1. Start by marinating the chicken in teriyaki sauce for at least 30 minutes to enhance the flavor.

2. Cut the vegetables into uniform sizes to ensure even cooking.

3. Heat a large skillet or wok over high heat and add oil before adding the chicken.

4. Cook the chicken until browned on all sides before removing from the pan.

5. Add the vegetables to the same pan and stir-fry until tender-crisp.

6. Return the chicken to the pan and pour in the teriyaki sauce, stirring to coat everything evenly.

7. Serve the stir-fry over rice or noodles for a complete meal. Adjust seasoning to taste.

Broiled tilapia with mango salsa

Ingredients:

- 4 tilapia fillets
- 2 ripe mangoes
- 1 red bell pepper
- 1/4 cup red onion
- 1/4 cup fresh cilantro
- 1 lime, juiced
- Salt and pepper to taste

Equipment:

1. Baking sheet
2. Mixing bowls
3. Whisk
4. Skillet
5. Chef's knife

Methods:

Step 1: Preheat broiler and line a baking sheet with foil.

Step 2: Season tilapia fillets with salt, pepper, and chili powder.

Step 3: Place fillets on the baking sheet and broil for 4-6 minutes per side, or until fish flakes easily with a fork.

Step 4: While the fish is cooking, prepare the mango salsa by mixing diced mango, red onion, jalapeno, cilantro, lime juice, and salt in a bowl.

Step 5: Serve the broiled tilapia topped with the mango salsa and enjoy!

Helpful Tips:

1. Preheat broiler and line a baking sheet with foil.

2. Season tilapia fillets with salt, pepper, and a squeeze of lemon juice.

3. Broil tilapia for 5-6 minutes per side, or until the fish flakes easily with a fork.

4. In a bowl, combine diced mango, red onion, jalapeno, cilantro, lime juice, and salt to make the salsa.

5. Serve broiled tilapia topped with mango salsa and a side of rice or quinoa. Enjoy!

Caprese salad with fresh basil and balsamic reduction

Ingredients:
- 2 large beefsteak tomatoes
- 8 oz fresh mozzarella cheese
- 1/4 cup balsamic vinegar
- 1/4 cup fresh basil leaves

Equipment:
1. Chef's knife
2. Cutting board
3. Mixing bowl
4. Tongs
5. Skillet

Methods:
Step 1: Slice ripe tomatoes and fresh mozzarella cheese into rounds.

Step 2: Arrange tomato and mozzarella slices on a serving platter, alternating between the two.

Step 3: Drizzle with olive oil and season with salt and pepper.

Step 4: Tear fresh basil leaves and scatter them over the top of the salad.

Step 5: In a small saucepan, heat balsamic vinegar over medium heat until it reduces by half.

Step 6: Drizzle the balsamic reduction over the salad just before serving.

Step 7: Enjoy your delicious Caprese salad with fresh basil and balsamic reduction!

Helpful Tips:
1. Start by slicing fresh, ripe tomatoes and creamy mozzarella cheese into equal thickness.

2. Arrange them in a circular pattern on a plate, alternating between tomato and cheese slices.

3. Drizzle with a high-quality balsamic reduction for a sweet and tangy flavor.

4. Garnish with freshly torn basil leaves for a burst of aromatic freshness.

5. Season with salt and pepper to taste, and serve immediately for the best flavor.

6. Consider adding a drizzle of extra virgin olive oil for an added touch of richness.

7. Customize with additional ingredients like pine nuts or avocado for a unique twist.

Pork tenderloin with cranberry relish

Ingredients:

- 1 pork tenderloin (1 lb)
- 1 cup fresh cranberries
- 1/2 cup sugar
- 1/4 cup orange juice
- Salt and pepper to taste

Equipment:

1. Knife
2. Cutting board
3. Frying pan
4. Mixing bowl
5. Serving platter

Methods:

Step 1: Preheat the oven to 425°F.

Step 2: Season the pork tenderloin with salt, pepper, and your favorite herbs.

Step 3: Place the pork tenderloin on a baking sheet and roast in the oven for 25-30 minutes, or until internal temperature reaches 145°F.

Step 4: While the pork is cooking, make the cranberry relish by combining cranberries, sugar, orange zest, and orange juice in a saucepan.

Step 5: Cook the cranberry relish over medium heat until the cranberries burst and the mixture thickens, about 10 minutes.

Step 6: Slice the pork tenderloin and serve with the cranberry relish. Enjoy!

Helpful Tips:

1. Preheat your oven to 425°F before starting to cook the pork tenderloin.

2. Season the pork tenderloin with salt, pepper, and olive oil before searing in a hot pan.

3. Sear the pork tenderloin on all sides until golden brown, then transfer to a baking dish.

4. Roast the pork tenderloin in the oven for about 20-25 minutes, or until it reaches an internal temperature of 145°F.

5. While the pork is cooking, prepare the cranberry relish by combining fresh cranberries, sugar, orange juice, and zest in a saucepan over medium heat.

6. Cook the cranberry relish until the cranberries burst and the mixture thickens, then serve over sliced pork tenderloin. Enjoy!

Lemon and herb marinated grilled chicken

Ingredients:

- 1 lb chicken breasts
- 1/4 cup lemon juice
- 2 tbsp olive oil
- 2 cloves garlic
- 1 tsp salt
- 1/2 tsp pepper
- 1 tbsp chopped herbs

Equipment:

1. Grill
2. Tongs
3. Mixing bowl
4. Whisk
5. Knife
6. Cutting board

Methods:

Step 1: In a bowl, mix together the lemon juice, olive oil, minced garlic, and chopped herbs to create the marinade.

Step 2: Place the chicken breasts in a resealable plastic bag and pour the marinade over them.

Step 3: Seal the bag and refrigerate for at least 30 minutes to allow the flavors to penetrate the chicken.

Step 4: Preheat the grill to medium-high heat and oil the grates to prevent sticking.

Step 5: Remove the chicken from the marinade and grill for about 6-8 minutes per side, or until the internal temperature reaches 165°F.

Step 6: Let the chicken rest for a few minutes before serving. Enjoy your lemon and herb marinated grilled chicken!

Helpful Tips:

1. Start by marinating the chicken in a mixture of lemon juice, olive oil, garlic, and herbs for at least 1 hour.

2. Preheat your grill to medium-high heat before adding the chicken.

3. Cook the chicken for about 6-8 minutes per side, or until it reaches an internal temperature of 165°F.

4. Be sure to let the chicken rest for a few minutes before serving to allow the juices to redistribute.

5. Garnish with fresh herbs and a squeeze of lemon before serving for added flavor.

Greek chicken souvlaki with tzatziki sauce

Ingredients:
- 1 lb chicken breast, cubed
- 1/4 cup olive oil
- 1/4 cup lemon juice
- 2 cloves garlic, minced
- 1 tsp dried oregano
- 1/2 cup Greek yogurt
- 1/4 cup cucumber, grated
- 1 tbsp lemon juice
- 1 clove garlic, minced

Equipment:
1. Mixing bowl
2. Grilling tongs
3. Skewers
4. Grater
5. Garlic press

Methods:
Step 1: Marinate chicken in olive oil, lemon juice, garlic, oregano, salt, and pepper for at least 1 hour.

Step 2: Skewer marinated chicken pieces on wooden or metal skewers.

Step 3: Grill chicken skewers over medium-high heat until cooked through and slightly charred, about 5-7 minutes per side.

Step 4: For tzatziki sauce, combine Greek yogurt, grated cucumber, garlic, lemon juice, dill, salt, and pepper in a bowl.

Step 5: Serve grilled chicken souvlaki with warm pita bread, sliced tomatoes, red onions, and tzatziki sauce on the side.

Step 6: Enjoy your delicious Greek chicken souvlaki with tzatziki sauce!

Helpful Tips:
1. Marinate chicken in olive oil, lemon juice, garlic, oregano, and salt for at least 1 hour.

2. Skewer marinated chicken and grill until cooked through, approximately 6-8 minutes per side.

3. For the tzatziki sauce, combine Greek yogurt, cucumber, garlic, dill, lemon juice, salt, and pepper in a bowl.

4. Refrigerate tzatziki sauce for at least 30 minutes before serving to allow flavors to meld.

5. Serve chicken souvlaki with warm pita bread, sliced tomatoes, red onions, and a generous dollop of tzatziki sauce on top. Enjoy!

Veggie egg white scramble with avocado

Ingredients:

- 8 egg whites
- 1/2 red bell pepper
- 1/2 green bell pepper
- 1/2 onion
- 1 avocado
- Salt and pepper
- Olive oil

Equipment:

1. Skillet
2. Whisk
3. Spatula
4. Knife
5. Cutting board

Methods:

Step 1: Heat a non-stick pan on medium heat and add 1 teaspoon of olive oil.

Step 2: Add 1/4 cup diced onions and sauté until translucent.

Step 3: Add 1/2 cup diced bell peppers and cook until slightly softened.

Step 4: Add 1/2 cup diced tomatoes and cook for another minute.

Step 5: Pour in 4 beaten egg whites and stir gently until cooked through.

Step 6: Season with salt, pepper, and any other desired seasonings.

Step 7: Remove from heat and mix in diced avocado.

Step 8: Serve hot and enjoy your veggie egg white scramble with avocado!

Helpful Tips:

1. Start by heating a non-stick skillet over medium heat.

2. Add diced bell peppers, onions, and any other vegetables of your choice to the skillet.

3. Cook the vegetables until they are tender, stirring occasionally.

4. In a separate bowl, whisk together the egg whites and season with salt and pepper.

5. Pour the egg white mixture over the cooked vegetables in the skillet.

6. Use a spatula to gently stir the eggs until they are cooked through.

7. Serve the scrambled eggs with sliced avocado on top for a creamy and nutritious finish.

8. Enjoy your healthy and filling veggie egg white scramble with avocado!

Spinach and artichoke stuffed mushrooms

Ingredients:
- 16 large mushrooms
- 1 cup chopped spinach
- 1/2 cup artichoke hearts
- 1/2 cup cream cheese

Equipment:
1. Knife
2. Cutting board
3. Mixing bowl
4. Baking sheet
5. Spoon
6. Oven

Methods:
Step 1: Preheat the oven to 375°F.

Step 2: Clean the mushrooms and remove the stems. Set aside.

Step 3: In a bowl, mix together chopped spinach, diced artichokes, cream cheese, shredded mozzarella, and parmesan cheese.

Step 4: Stuff each mushroom cap with the mixture and place on a baking sheet.

Step 5: Bake for 20-25 minutes, or until mushrooms are cooked through.

Step 6: Serve hot and enjoy your delicious spinach and artichoke stuffed mushrooms!

Helpful Tips:
1. Preheat your oven to 375°F before starting the recipe.

2. Remove the stems from the mushrooms and chop them finely for the filling.

3. Sauté the chopped mushroom stems, garlic, spinach, and artichokes in olive oil until they are cooked through.

4. Season the filling with salt, pepper, and any other desired seasonings.

5. Fill the mushroom caps with the spinach and artichoke mixture, pressing it down firmly.

6. Place the stuffed mushrooms on a baking sheet and bake for 20-25 minutes, or until they are cooked through.

7. Serve hot as a delicious appetizer or side dish. Enjoy!

Baked balsamic chicken with Brussels sprouts

Ingredients:

- 4 chicken breasts
- 1/2 cup balsamic vinegar
- 2 tbsp olive oil
- 1 tsp dried thyme
- 1 lb Brussels sprouts

Equipment:

1. Baking dish
2. Sheet pan
3. Mixing bowl
4. Whisk
5. Tongs

Methods:

Step 1: Preheat the oven to 400°F.

Step 2: Place Brussels sprouts on a baking sheet, drizzle with olive oil, salt, and pepper, and toss to coat.

Step 3: In a bowl, mix balsamic vinegar, honey, garlic, and Dijon mustard.

Step 4: Place chicken breasts on the baking sheet with the Brussels sprouts.

Step 5: Brush the balsamic mixture onto the chicken breasts.

Step 6: Bake in the preheated oven for 25-30 minutes, or until the chicken is cooked through.

Step 7: Serve hot and enjoy your delicious baked balsamic chicken with Brussels sprouts.

Helpful Tips:

1. Preheat your oven to 400°F.

2. Clean and trim the Brussels sprouts, then cut them in half.

3. Season the chicken thighs with salt, pepper, and garlic powder.

4. In a large bowl, toss the Brussels sprouts with olive oil, balsamic vinegar, salt, pepper, and minced garlic.

5. Place the chicken thighs in a baking dish and spread the Brussels sprouts around them.

6. Bake for 25-30 minutes, or until the chicken is cooked through.

7. For extra flavor, drizzle with extra balsamic vinegar before serving. Enjoy!

Quinoa and black bean stuffed peppers

Ingredients:

- 1 cup quinoa
- 1 can black beans
- 4 bell peppers
- 1 cup shredded cheese
- 1 onion, diced
- 2 cloves garlic
- 1 tsp cumin
- 1 tsp chili powder

Equipment:

1. cutting board
2. knife
3. skillet
4. spoon
5. baking dish

Methods:

Step 1: Preheat the oven to 375°F.

Step 2: Cook quinoa according to package instructions.

Step 3: In a skillet, sauté onions, garlic, and bell peppers until softened.

Step 4: Add black beans, corn, and spices to the skillet and cook until heated through.

Step 5: Combine cooked quinoa with the black bean mixture.

Step 6: Cut the tops off the peppers and remove seeds.

Step 7: Stuff the peppers with the quinoa mixture.

Step 8: Place peppers in a baking dish and cover with foil.

Step 9: Bake for 25-30 minutes or until peppers are tender.

Step 10: Serve hot and enjoy!

Helpful Tips:

1. Preheat your oven to 375°F before starting
2. Rinse quinoa under cold water to remove bitter coating

3. Cook quinoa according to package instructions

4. Cut the tops off bell peppers and remove seeds

5. Mix cooked quinoa with black beans, corn, diced tomatoes, and spices

6. Stuff the mixture into the bell peppers

7. Place stuffed peppers in a baking dish and cover with foil

8. Bake for 25-30 minutes until peppers are tender

9. Top with shredded cheese or avocado before serving

10. Enjoy your nutritious and flavorful quinoa and black bean stuffed peppers!

Grilled shrimp and vegetable skewers

Ingredients:

- 1 pound shrimp
- 2 bell peppers
- 1 zucchini
- 1 red onion
- 1/4 cup olive oil
- 2 cloves garlic
- Salt and pepper to taste

Equipment:

1. Skewers
2. Grill pan
3. Tongs
4. Cutting board
5. Knife

Methods:

Step 1: Soak wooden skewers in water for 30 minutes.

Step 2: Preheat grill to medium-high heat.

Step 3: In a bowl, toss shrimp and vegetables with olive oil, salt, and pepper.

Step 4: Thread shrimp and vegetables onto skewers.

Step 5: Place skewers on the grill and cook for 2-3 minutes per side, until shrimp is pink and vegetables are tender.

Step 6: Remove skewers from grill and serve hot.

Step 7: Optional: garnish with chopped parsley and a squeeze of lemon juice. Enjoy your delicious grilled shrimp and vegetable skewers!

Helpful Tips:

1. Soak wooden skewers in water for at least 30 minutes to prevent burning.

2. Marinate shrimp in a combination of olive oil, garlic, lemon juice, and seasonings for at least 20 minutes.

3. Alternate threading shrimp and your favorite vegetables onto skewers for even cooking.

4. Preheat grill to medium-high heat and lightly oil the grates to prevent sticking.

5. Grill skewers for 2-3 minutes per side, or until shrimp is opaque and vegetables are tender.

6. Serve hot with a squeeze of fresh lemon juice and a sprinkle of chopped herbs for extra flavor. Enjoy!

Sautéed tilapia with lemon and garlic

Ingredients:
- 4 tilapia fillets
- 2 cloves of garlic, minced
- 2 tablespoons of olive oil
- 1 lemon, juiced
- Salt and pepper to taste

Equipment:
1. Skillet
2. Tongs
3. Lemon zester
4. Garlic press
5. Spatula

Methods:
Step 1: Season tilapia fillets with salt and pepper.

Step 2: Heat olive oil in a pan over medium heat.

Step 3: Add minced garlic to the pan and sauté until fragrant.

Step 4: Place seasoned tilapia fillets in the pan and cook for 3-4 minutes on each side.

Step 5: Squeeze fresh lemon juice over the fillets.

Step 6: Add a knob of butter to the pan and let it melt and coat the fish.

Step 7: Remove the tilapia from the pan and serve hot, garnished with fresh parsley.

Step 8: Enjoy your sautéed tilapia with lemon and garlic!

Helpful Tips:
1. Start by patting the tilapia fillets dry with a paper towel to prevent them from getting mushy while cooking.

2. Heat a skillet over medium-high heat and add a bit of olive oil to coat the bottom of the pan.

3. Season the fillets with salt, pepper, and a sprinkle of garlic powder before adding them to the skillet.

4. Cook the fish for 3-4 minutes on each side, or until it easily flakes with a fork.

5. Squeeze fresh lemon juice over the fish and sprinkle with minced garlic before serving.

6. Enjoy your sautéed tilapia with a side of steamed vegetables or a fresh green salad.

Lemon herb chicken skewers with tzatziki sauce

Ingredients:
- 1 lb boneless, skinless chicken breast
- 1 lemon, juiced and zested
- 2 cloves garlic, minced
- 1 tsp dried oregano
- 1/4 cup olive oil
- 1 cup Greek yogurt
- 1 cucumber, grated
- 1 tbsp fresh dill

Equipment:
1. Skewers
2. Grilling pan
3. Mixing bowl
4. Tongs
5. Cutting board
6. Knife

Methods:
Step 1: In a large bowl, mix olive oil, lemon juice, garlic, thyme, rosemary, salt, and pepper.

Step 2: Cut boneless, skinless chicken breasts into 1-inch cubes and add to the marinade. Coat well and refrigerate for at least 30 minutes.

Step 3: Preheat the grill to medium-high heat.

Step 4: Thread marinated chicken cubes onto skewers.

Step 5: Grill skewers for 10-12 minutes, turning occasionally, until chicken is cooked through and has nice grill marks.

Step 6: In a small bowl, mix Greek yogurt, grated cucumber, garlic, lemon juice, and dill to make tzatziki sauce.

Step 7: Serve chicken skewers with tzatziki sauce on the side. Enjoy!

Helpful Tips:

1. Marinate the chicken in a mixture of lemon juice, olive oil, garlic, and herbs for at least 30 minutes to enhance the flavor.

2. Soak wooden skewers in water for at least 30 minutes to prevent burning during grilling.

3. Alternate threading chicken pieces with bell peppers, onions, and cherry tomatoes for a balanced skewer.

4. Grill the skewers over medium heat, turning occasionally, until the chicken is cooked through and slightly charred.

5. Mix together Greek yogurt, cucumber, garlic, lemon juice, and dill for a refreshing tzatziki sauce to serve on the side. Enjoy!

Cottage cheese and fruit bowl

Ingredients:

- 2 cups cottage cheese
- 1 cup sliced strawberries
- 1 cup blueberries
- 1/2 cup granola

Equipment:

1. Spatula
2. Whisk
3. Chef's knife
4. Cutting board
5. Mixing bowls

Methods:

Step 1: Gather your ingredients - cottage cheese, mixed fruits (such as berries, mango, and banana), honey, and granola.

Step 2: Wash and chop the fruits into bite-sized pieces.

Step 3: In a bowl, layer the cottage cheese followed by the mixed fruits.

Step 4: Drizzle honey over the top for added sweetness.

Step 5: Sprinkle granola on top for a crunchy texture.

Step 6: Mix all the ingredients together gently.

Step 7: Serve immediately and enjoy your cottage cheese and fruit bowl as a healthy and delicious snack or breakfast.

Helpful Tips:

1. Choose fresh, ripe fruits like berries, mangoes, or peaches to complement the creamy texture of cottage cheese.

2. Cut the fruits into bite-sized pieces for easier eating and better presentation.

3. Try adding a drizzle of honey or a sprinkle of cinnamon for extra flavor.

4. Consider mixing in some nuts or seeds for added crunch and protein.

5. Serve the cottage cheese and fruit bowl chilled for a refreshing and satisfying snack or breakfast.

Roasted Brussels sprouts with balsamic glaze

Ingredients:
- 1 lb Brussels sprouts
- 2 tbsp olive oil
- 2 tbsp balsamic vinegar
- 1 tbsp honey

Equipment:
1. Baking sheet
2. Mixing bowl
3. Whisk
4. Saucepan
5. Basting brush

Methods:
Step 1: Preheat the oven to 400°F.

Step 2: Trim the ends off the Brussels sprouts and cut them in half.

Step 3: Toss the Brussels sprouts with olive oil, salt, and pepper on a baking sheet.

Step 4: Roast in the oven for 25-30 minutes, or until they are golden brown and crispy.

Step 5: While the Brussels sprouts are roasting, make the balsamic glaze by simmering balsamic vinegar in a saucepan until it thickens.

Step 6: Drizzle the balsamic glaze over the roasted Brussels sprouts before serving.

Step 7: Enjoy your delicious roasted Brussels sprouts with balsamic glaze!

Helpful Tips:
1. Preheat your oven to 400°F to ensure even cooking.
2. Trim the ends of the Brussels sprouts and remove any brown outer leaves.
3. Cut the Brussels sprouts in half for quicker cooking and easier serving.
4. Toss the Brussels sprouts with olive oil, salt, and pepper before spreading them out on a baking sheet.

5. Roast the Brussels sprouts for 25-30 minutes, shaking the pan halfway through to ensure even browning.

6. While the Brussels sprouts are roasting, prepare the balsamic glaze by simmering balsamic vinegar and honey in a small saucepan until thickened.

7. Drizzle the balsamic glaze over the roasted Brussels sprouts before serving for a delicious finishing touch.

Chicken and vegetable kabobs with Greek yogurt marinade

Ingredients:
- 1 lb of chicken breast, cut into chunks
- 1 red bell pepper, cut into squares
- 1 zucchini, sliced
- 1/2 cup Greek yogurt
- 1 tbsp olive oil
- 1 tbsp lemon juice
- 2 cloves garlic, minced
- Salt and pepper to taste

Equipment:
1. Skewers
2. Mixing bowl
3. Knife
4. Cutting board
5. Grill or grill pan

Methods:
Step 1: Cut boneless, skinless chicken breasts into bite-sized pieces.

Step 2: In a bowl, mix plain Greek yogurt with minced garlic, lemon juice, olive oil, and herbs like oregano and parsley.

Step 3: Add the chicken pieces to the marinade, making sure they are fully coated.

Step 4: Cover and refrigerate the chicken for at least 2 hours.

Step 5: Preheat the grill on medium heat.

Step 6: Thread the marinated chicken pieces onto skewers, alternating with sliced bell peppers, onions, and cherry tomatoes.

Step 7: Grill the kabobs for 10-15 minutes, turning occasionally until the chicken is cooked through.

Step 8: Serve hot and enjoy!

Helpful Tips:

1. Cut chicken and vegetables into uniform pieces for even cooking.

2. Soak wooden skewers in water for at least 30 minutes before threading ingredients to prevent burning.

3. Marinate chicken in Greek yogurt, garlic, lemon juice, and herbs for at least 2 hours for maximum flavor.

4. Preheat grill to medium-high heat before cooking the kabobs.

5. Thread chicken and vegetables onto skewers, alternating for even distribution.

6. Grill kabobs for 10-15 minutes, turning occasionally, until chicken is cooked through.

7. Serve kabobs with a side of rice or pita bread and extra Greek yogurt sauce for dipping. Enjoy!

Stuffed acorn squash with quinoa and cranberries

Ingredients:
- 2 acorn squash
- 1 cup quinoa
- 1/2 cup dried cranberries
- 1/4 cup chopped walnuts
- 1/4 cup chopped parsley
- Olive oil, salt, pepper

Equipment:
1. Knife
2. Cutting board
3. Mixing bowl
4. Baking sheet
5. Spoon
6. Oven mitts

Methods:
Step 1: Preheat oven to 375°F.

Step 2: Cut an acorn squash in half and remove the seeds.

Step 3: Place the squash halves on a baking sheet, cut side up.

Step 4: Drizzle with olive oil and season with salt and pepper.

Step 5: Bake for 30 minutes or until squash is tender.

Step 6: Cook quinoa according to package instructions.

Step 7: In a bowl, mix cooked quinoa with dried cranberries, chopped pecans, and a drizzle of maple syrup.

Step 8: Fill the cooked squash halves with the quinoa mixture.

Step 9: Bake for an additional 10 minutes.

Step 10: Serve and enjoy your stuffed acorn squash with quinoa and cranberries!

Helpful Tips:
1. Preheat oven to 400°F and line a baking sheet with parchment paper.

2. Cut acorn squash in half and scoop out the seeds.

3. Season squash with olive oil, salt, and pepper before roasting.

4. Cook quinoa according to package instructions and mix in dried cranberries.

5. Stuff the cooked quinoa mixture into the roasted acorn squash halves.

6. Top with chopped nuts or cheese for added flavor.

7. Bake for an additional 10-15 minutes until squash is easily pierced with a fork.

8. Serve hot and enjoy this delicious and nutritious meal!

Spaghetti squash with turkey bolognese sauce

Ingredients:
- 1 medium spaghetti squash
- 1 lb ground turkey
- 1 can crushed tomatoes
- 1 onion
- 2 cloves garlic
- 1 tsp dried oregano
- Salt and pepper to taste

Equipment:
1. Knife
2. Cutting board
3. Saucepan
4. Wooden spoon
5. Colander
6. Serving bowl

Methods:
Step 1: Preheat the oven to 400 degrees F.

Step 2: Cut the spaghetti squash in half lengthwise and remove the seeds.

Step 3: Place the squash halves cut side down on a baking sheet and bake for 40-45 minutes, or until the squash is tender.

Step 4: While the squash is baking, heat olive oil in a large skillet over medium heat.

Step 5: Add ground turkey to the skillet and cook until browned.

Step 6: Stir in chopped onions, garlic, carrots, and celery and cook until vegetables are softened.

Step 7: Add crushed tomatoes, tomato paste, and seasonings to the skillet and simmer for 20 minutes.

Step 8: Once the squash is done baking, use a fork to scrape the insides into "spaghetti" strands.

Step 9: Serve the squash with the turkey bolognese sauce on top. Enjoy!

Helpful Tips:

1. Start by preheating the oven to 400°F and cutting the spaghetti squash in half lengthwise.

2. Scoop out the seeds and brush the inside with olive oil, then sprinkle with salt and pepper.

3. Place the squash halves cut side down on a baking sheet and bake for 30-40 minutes until tender.

4. While the squash is baking, prepare the bolognese sauce by browning ground turkey in a skillet with chopped onions, garlic, and diced tomatoes.

5. Season with Italian herbs, salt, and pepper, then let simmer for 15-20 minutes.

6. Once the squash is done, use a fork to scrape out the "spaghetti" strands and top with the bolognese sauce before serving. Enjoy!

Grilled chicken Caesar salad with light dressing

Ingredients:
- 4 chicken breasts
- 1 head of romaine lettuce
- 1 cup of cherry tomatoes
- 1/2 cup of shredded parmesan cheese
- 1/2 cup of croutons
- 1/4 cup of Caesar dressing
- Salt and pepper to taste

Equipment:
1. Grill
2. Mixing bowl
3. Kitchen tongs
4. Salad spinner
5. Cutting board
6. Chef's knife

Methods:
Step 1: Preheat the grill to medium-high heat.

Step 2: Season chicken breast with salt, pepper, and garlic powder.

Step 3: Grill the chicken breast for 6-7 minutes per side, or until fully cooked.

Step 4: Let the chicken rest for a few minutes before slicing it into strips.

Step 5: In a large bowl, toss together romaine lettuce, cherry tomatoes, and croutons.

Step 6: Add the sliced chicken to the salad.

Step 7: In a small bowl, whisk together light Caesar dressing, lemon juice, and grated Parmesan cheese.

Step 8: Drizzle the dressing over the salad and toss to combine.

Step 9: Serve the grilled chicken Caesar salad with extra Parmesan cheese on top. Enjoy!

Helpful Tips:

1. Marinade the chicken in a combination of olive oil, lemon juice, minced garlic, and Italian seasoning for at least 30 minutes before grilling.

2. Use a mix of romaine lettuce and other greens for a more flavorful salad base.

3. Toast some croutons in the oven or on the stovetop for added crunch.

4. Make a lighter Caesar dressing by using Greek yogurt or light mayo as a base, and adding garlic, lemon juice, Dijon mustard, and Parmesan cheese.

5. Grill the chicken over medium-high heat until it reaches an internal temperature of 165°F, then let it rest before slicing and topping your salad. Enjoy!

Egg white frittata with spinach and tomatoes

Ingredients:
- 8 egg whites
- 2 cups spinach
- 1 cup cherry tomatoes
- Salt and pepper

Equipment:
1. Skillet
2. Whisk
3. Spatula
4. Cutting board
5. Knife
6. Mixing bowl

Methods:
Step 1: Preheat the oven to 350°F.

Step 2: In a skillet, sauté chopped spinach and tomatoes until wilted.

Step 3: In a mixing bowl, whisk together egg whites, salt, pepper, and garlic powder.

Step 4: Pour the egg white mixture over the sautéed vegetables in the skillet.

Step 5: Cook on the stovetop for 5 minutes without stirring.

Step 6: Transfer the skillet to the preheated oven and bake for 10-15 minutes, until the frittata is set.

Step 7: Remove from the oven and let it cool slightly before slicing and serving. Enjoy your egg white frittata with spinach and tomatoes!

Helpful Tips:
1. Beat the egg whites until stiff peaks form for a fluffy texture.

2. Cook the spinach and tomatoes beforehand to prevent excess moisture in the frittata.

3. Use a non-stick skillet to avoid sticking and make clean-up easier.

4. Season well with salt, pepper, and herbs for extra flavor.

5. Use low heat and cover the skillet to ensure even cooking throughout.

6. Top with cheese or fresh herbs for a finishing touch before serving.

Grilled salmon with lemon dill sauce

Ingredients:

- 4 salmon fillets
- 1/4 cup lemon juice
- 2 tbsp olive oil
- 2 tsp dill
- Salt and pepper to taste
- 1 minced garlic clove

Equipment:

1. Grill pan
2. Tongs
3. Spatula
4. Lemon juicer
5. Mixing bowl
6. Whisk

Methods:

Step 1: Preheat the grill to medium-high heat.

Step 2: Season the salmon fillets with salt and pepper.

Step 3: Place the salmon on the grill, skin-side down.

Step 4: Grill the salmon for about 4-5 minutes per side, or until cooked through.

Step 5: In a small bowl, mix together mayonnaise, lemon juice, dill, and garlic.

Step 6: Spoon the lemon dill sauce over the grilled salmon.

Step 7: Serve the grilled salmon with additional lemon slices and dill for garnish.

Step 8: Enjoy your delicious grilled salmon with lemon dill sauce!

Helpful Tips:

1. Start by preheating your grill to medium-high heat for optimal cooking temperature.

2. Season your salmon fillets with salt, pepper, and a drizzle of olive oil before placing them on the grill.

3. Cook the salmon skin-side down for 4-5 minutes, then carefully flip and cook for an additional 3-4 minutes.

4. While the salmon is cooking, mix together mayonnaise, lemon juice, fresh dill, and garlic to create a flavorful sauce.

5. Serve the grilled salmon hot off the grill with a generous spoonful of the lemon dill sauce on top. Enjoy with your favorite side dishes!

Turkey and vegetable stir-fry with ginger soy sauce

Ingredients:
- 1 lb turkey breast, sliced
- 2 cups mixed vegetables
- 2 tbsp soy sauce
- 1 tsp ginger, grated
- 1 tbsp vegetable oil

Equipment:
1. Wok
2. Spatula
3. Knife
4. Cutting board
5. Mixing bowl

Methods:
Step 1: Heat 1 tablespoon of vegetable oil in a large skillet or wok over medium-high heat.

Step 2: Add 1 pound of thinly sliced turkey breast and cook until browned and cooked through.

Step 3: Remove turkey from the skillet and set aside.

Step 4: In the same skillet, add 1 tablespoon of minced ginger and 2 cloves of minced garlic. Cook for 1-2 minutes until fragrant.

Step 5: Add 2 cups of sliced mixed vegetables (such as bell peppers, carrots, and snap peas) and stir-fry for 3-4 minutes.

Step 6: Return the turkey to the skillet and add 1/4 cup of soy sauce.

Step 7: Cook for another 2-3 minutes until everything is heated through.

Step 8: Serve the turkey and vegetable stir-fry over cooked rice and enjoy!

Helpful Tips:
1. Begin by marinating the turkey slices in a mixture of soy sauce, ginger, garlic, and a touch of sugar for at least 30 minutes.

2. Heat a wok or large skillet over high heat and add oil. Stir-fry the marinated turkey until cooked through.

3. Remove the turkey from the pan and set aside.

4. In the same pan, stir-fry your favorite combination of fresh vegetables such as bell peppers, snap peas, broccoli, and carrots until crisp-tender.

5. Return the turkey to the pan and add a homemade or store-bought ginger soy sauce. Cook for an additional minute.

6. Serve the flavorful stir-fry over steamed rice or noodles. Enjoy!

Greek yogurt and fruit smoothie

Ingredients:

- 2 cups Greek yogurt
- 2 cups mixed fruits
- 1/4 cup honey
- 1/2 cup almond milk
- 1 teaspoon vanilla extract

Equipment:

1. Knife
2. Cutting board
3. Measuring cups
4. Mixing bowls
5. Wooden spoon

Methods:

Step 1: Gather your ingredients, including Greek yogurt, your choice of fruits (such as berries or bananas), honey or agave nectar, and some ice cubes.

Step 2: Place the Greek yogurt, fruits, honey or agave nectar, and ice cubes into a blender.

Step 3: Blend the ingredients on high speed until a smooth consistency is reached.

Step 4: Taste the smoothie and adjust sweetness if needed by adding more honey or agave nectar.

Step 5: Pour the smoothie into a glass and enjoy! Optional: garnish with fresh fruit slices or a sprinkle of chia seeds.

Helpful Tips:

1. Start by blending 1 cup of Greek yogurt with 1 cup of frozen fruits (like berries or bananas) for a creamy texture.

2. Add a splash of liquid (such as almond milk or orange juice) to help the ingredients blend smoothly.

3. Sweeten the smoothie with honey, maple syrup, or a few dates for natural sweetness.

4. For extra nutrition, add a handful of spinach or kale to sneak in some greens.

5. Customize your smoothie by adding in extras like chia seeds, nut butter, or protein powder.

6. Blend everything until smooth and enjoy as a refreshing and nutritious snack or breakfast option.

Tofu and vegetable curry with brown rice

Ingredients:
- 1 block of tofu, diced
- 2 cups mixed vegetables
- 1 can coconut milk
- 2 tbsp curry paste
- 1 cup brown rice

Equipment:
1. Saucepan
2. Wooden spoon
3. Chef's knife
4. Cutting board
5. Stirring spoon
6. Rice cooker

Methods:
Step 1: Press tofu to remove excess moisture, then cut into cubes.

Step 2: Heat a large skillet or wok over medium-high heat and add oil.

Step 3: Add chopped onions, garlic, and ginger to the skillet and sauté until fragrant.

Step 4: Add tofu cubes and cook until browned on all sides.

Step 5: Stir in curry paste, coconut milk, and vegetable broth.

Step 6: Add sliced bell peppers, broccoli, and carrots to the skillet.

Step 7: Cook until vegetables are tender.

Step 8: Serve tofu and vegetable curry over brown rice and garnish with fresh cilantro.

Helpful Tips:
1. Press the tofu before cooking to remove excess moisture and improve texture.

2. Use firm or extra firm tofu for best results in the curry.

3. Cut tofu into bite-sized cubes for even cooking.

4. Sauté onions, garlic, and ginger in a large saucepan with oil until fragrant.

5. Add your favorite vegetables such as bell peppers, zucchini, and carrots to the curry.

6. Stir in coconut milk, curry paste, soy sauce, and vegetable broth for flavor.

7. Simmer the curry until vegetables are tender and tofu has absorbed the flavors.

8. Serve over cooked brown rice for a nutritious and satisfying meal.

Baked cod with garlic herb butter

Ingredients:
- 4 cod fillets
- 4 cloves of garlic, minced
- 4 tbsp of butter
- 1 tbsp of fresh herbs
- Salt and pepper to taste

Equipment:
1. Baking dish
2. Basting brush
3. Garlic press
4. Mixing bowl
5. Serving spoon

Methods:
Step 1: Preheat the oven to 400°F.

Step 2: Place cod fillets in a baking dish.

Step 3: In a small bowl, mix softened butter with minced garlic and herbs (such as parsley, thyme, and dill).

Step 4: Spread the garlic herb butter mixture over the cod fillets.

Step 5: Squeeze fresh lemon juice over the fillets and season with salt and pepper.

Step 6: Cover the baking dish with foil and bake for 15-20 minutes, or until the fish is cooked through and flakes easily with a fork.

Step 7: Serve the baked cod with a side of steamed vegetables or a fresh salad. Enjoy!

Helpful Tips:
1. Preheat your oven to 400°F before starting to cook.

2. Season the cod with salt, pepper, and a squeeze of lemon juice before baking.

3. Make the garlic herb butter by mixing melted butter with minced garlic, chopped parsley, and a pinch of salt.

4. Spread the garlic herb butter over the top of the cod fillets.

5. Bake the cod in the preheated oven for about 15-20 minutes, or until the fish flakes easily with a fork.

6. Serve the baked cod hot with a side of your favorite veggies or salad. Enjoy!

Avocado and black bean salad with lime dressing

Ingredients:
- 2 avocados (peeled, pitted, and diced)
- 1 can black beans (drained and rinsed)
- 1/4 cup red onion (finely chopped)
- 1/4 cup fresh cilantro (chopped)
- Juice of 2 limes
- 2 tbsp olive oil
- Salt and pepper to taste

Equipment:
1. Mixing bowls
2. Whisk
3. Cutting board
4. Knife
5. Salad spinner

Methods:
Step 1: In a large bowl, combine 1 can of drained and rinsed black beans with 2 diced avocados.

Step 2: Add 1 diced red bell pepper, 1/4 cup chopped red onion, and 1/4 cup chopped fresh cilantro to the bowl.

Step 3: In a separate small bowl, whisk together 3 tablespoons of olive oil, the juice of 2 limes, 1 minced garlic clove, 1 teaspoon of cumin, and salt and pepper to taste.

Step 4: Pour the dressing over the salad and gently toss to combine.

Step 5: Serve chilled and enjoy your avocado and black bean salad with lime dressing!

Helpful Tips:
1. Start by rinsing and draining a can of black beans and chop up a ripe avocado.

2. In a bowl, combine the black beans, avocado, fresh corn kernels, diced tomatoes, and chopped red onion.

3. In a separate bowl, whisk together lime juice, olive oil, minced garlic, salt, and pepper to create the dressing.

4. Pour the dressing over the salad and toss gently to coat all the ingredients.

5. Let the salad sit for at least 15 minutes to allow the flavors to meld together before serving.

6. Garnish with fresh cilantro or parsley before serving for added flavor and freshness.

7. Enjoy your healthy and delicious avocado and black bean salad with lime dressing!

Turkey and avocado wrap with mixed greens

Ingredients:
- 1 lb cooked turkey slices
- 2 avocados, sliced
- 4 large whole wheat wraps
- 2 cups mixed greens

Equipment:
1. Knife
2. Cutting board
3. Mixing bowl
4. Frying pan
5. Spatula

Methods:
Step 1: Lay out a whole grain tortilla on a clean surface

Step 2: Spread a layer of mashed avocado on the tortilla

Step 3: Layer sliced turkey on top of the avocado

Step 4: Add a handful of mixed greens on top of the turkey

Step 5: Sprinkle with salt and pepper to taste

Step 6: Roll up the tortilla tightly, tucking in the sides as you go

Step 7: Cut the wrap in half diagonally for serving

Step 8: Enjoy your delicious and nutritious turkey and avocado wrap with mixed greens!

Helpful Tips:
1. Start by preparing all your ingredients - sliced turkey, ripe avocado, mixed greens, and any additional toppings.

2. Lay out a large whole wheat or spinach wrap on a clean surface.

3. Layer the turkey slices on the wrap, followed by slices of avocado and a generous handful of mixed greens.

4. Drizzle with your favorite dressing or spread, such as ranch or honey mustard.

5. Carefully fold the sides of the wrap in and then roll tightly from one end to the other.

6. Use a sharp knife to slice the wrap in half for easy serving.

7. Enjoy your delicious and nutritious turkey and avocado wrap with mixed greens!

Grilled chicken and vegetable burrito bowl

Ingredients:
- 1 lb chicken breast
- 1 bell pepper
- 1 onion
- 1 zucchini
- 1 cup corn
- 1 tsp cumin
- 1 tsp paprika
- 1/2 tsp garlic powder
- 1/4 cup olive oil
- 1 cup cooked rice
- 1/2 cup salsa
- 1/2 cup shredded cheese

Equipment:
1. Grill pan
2. Cutting board
3. Knife
4. Mixing bowl
5. Tongs
6. Serving bowl

Methods:
Step 1: Marinate chicken breasts in a mixture of olive oil, lime juice, garlic, cumin, and chili powder for at least 30 minutes.

Step 2: Preheat a grill pan over medium-high heat and grill chicken for 6-8 minutes on each side, until fully cooked.

Step 3: Meanwhile, chop bell peppers, red onion, and zucchini and sauté in a separate pan with olive oil until tender.

Step 4: Assemble burrito bowls by layering cooked quinoa or rice, grilled chicken, sautéed vegetables, black beans, avocado slices, and a drizzle of Greek yogurt or salsa on top.

Step 5: Serve hot and enjoy!

Helpful Tips:

1. Start by marinating the chicken in a mix of oil, lime juice, garlic, and your favorite spices for extra flavor.

2. Preheat your grill to medium-high heat before cooking the chicken to ensure even cooking.

3. Use a grill basket or skewers to cook your vegetables alongside the chicken for easy grilling.

4. Let the chicken rest for a few minutes before slicing it to retain its juices and tenderness.

5. Assemble your burrito bowl with cooked rice, grilled chicken, veggies, avocado, salsa, and a drizzle of dressing for a delicious and satisfying meal. Enjoy!

Baked sweet potato fries with garlic aioli

Ingredients:
- 2 large sweet potatoes
- 2 cloves of garlic
- 1/4 cup mayonnaise
- 1/2 tsp lemon juice
- Salt and pepper to taste

Equipment:
1. Baking sheet
2. Chef's knife
3. Mixing bowl
4. Whisk
5. Pot
6. Spatula

Methods:
Step 1: Preheat oven to 425°F and line a baking sheet with parchment paper.

Step 2: Peel and cut sweet potatoes into evenly sized fries.

Step 3: Toss sweet potato fries in olive oil, salt, pepper, and any desired seasonings.

Step 4: Spread fries in a single layer on the prepared baking sheet.

Step 5: Bake for 25-30 minutes, flipping halfway through, until fries are crispy and golden brown.

Step 6: While fries are baking, prepare the garlic aioli by combining mayonnaise, minced garlic, lemon juice, salt, and pepper.

Step 7: Serve sweet potato fries with the garlic aioli for dipping. Enjoy!

Helpful Tips:
1. Preheat your oven to 425°F and line a baking sheet with parchment paper.

2. Cut sweet potatoes into thin strips for even cooking.

3. Toss sweet potato strips with olive oil, salt, pepper, and any desired spices (paprika, cumin, etc.).

4. Spread sweet potatoes in a single layer on the baking sheet.

5. Bake for 25-30 minutes, flipping halfway through, until crispy and golden brown.

6. While fries are baking, make the garlic aioli by combining mayo, minced garlic, lemon juice, salt, and pepper.

7. Serve hot sweet potato fries with the creamy garlic aioli for dipping. Enjoy!

Seared tuna steak with mango salsa

Ingredients:
- 4 tuna steaks
- 1 ripe mango
- 1 red onion
- 1 jalapeño pepper
- 1 lime
- 1/4 cup cilantro
- Salt and pepper to taste

Equipment:
1. Chef's knife
2. Cutting board
3. Skillet
4. Tongs
5. Mixing bowl

Methods:
Step 1: Season the tuna steak with salt and pepper.

Step 2: Heat a pan over high heat with a little bit of oil.

Step 3: Sear the tuna steak for 1-2 minutes on each side for a rare cook.

Step 4: Remove the tuna from the pan and let it rest for a few minutes.

Step 5: In a bowl, mix diced mango, red onion, cilantro, lime juice, and a pinch of salt.

Step 6: Slice the tuna steak and serve it with the mango salsa on top.

Step 7: Enjoy your delicious seared tuna steak with mango salsa!

Helpful Tips:
1. Season the tuna steak generously with salt and pepper before searing.

2. Use a hot skillet or grill to quickly sear the tuna, around 1-2 minutes per side for a rare to medium-rare cook.

3. Prepare the mango salsa by combining diced mango, red onion, cucumber, jalapeno, cilantro, lime juice, and salt in a bowl.

4. Let the seared tuna rest for a few minutes before slicing to allow the juices to redistribute.

5. Serve the seared tuna steak with the mango salsa on top for a fresh and flavorful dish. Enjoy!

Kale and quinoa salad with lemon vinaigrette

Ingredients:
- 1 bunch of kale
- 1 cup of quinoa
- 1 lemon
- Olive oil
- Salt and pepper

Equipment:
1. Mixing bowl
2. Whisk
3. Knife
4. Cutting board
5. Salad spinner

Methods:
Step 1: Cook 1 cup of quinoa according to package instructions and let cool.

Step 2: Wash and chop 1 bunch of kale into bite-sized pieces.

Step 3: Massage kale with 1 tbsp of olive oil and a pinch of salt to soften.

Step 4: In a small bowl, whisk together 1/4 cup of olive oil, 2 tbsp of lemon juice, 1 minced garlic clove, and salt and pepper to taste for the vinaigrette.

Step 5: In a large bowl, toss together the cooked quinoa, massaged kale, 1/2 cup of cherry tomatoes, 1/4 cup of chopped almonds, and the lemon vinaigrette.

Step 6: Serve and enjoy!

Helpful Tips:
1. Rinse the quinoa well before cooking to remove any bitter taste.

2. Cook the quinoa according to package instructions, using either water or vegetable broth for added flavor.

3. Massage the kale with a bit of olive oil before adding it to the salad to help soften its texture.

4. Add a variety of colorful vegetables like cherry tomatoes, red bell peppers, and shredded carrots for added texture and flavor.

5. Make sure to thoroughly mix the lemon vinaigrette before drizzling it over the salad for even distribution of flavors.

Teriyaki turkey and vegetable stir-fry

Ingredients:
- 1 lb turkey breast, sliced
- 1 red bell pepper, sliced
- 1 yellow bell pepper, sliced
- 1 cup teriyaki sauce

Equipment:
1. Wok
2. Wooden spoon
3. Knife
4. Cutting board
5. Tongs

Methods:
Step 1: Marinate turkey strips in teriyaki sauce for 30 minutes.

Step 2: Heat a wok or large skillet over medium-high heat and add vegetable oil.

Step 3: Add marinated turkey strips and stir-fry until cooked through.

Step 4: Remove turkey from skillet and set aside.

Step 5: Add sliced vegetables such as bell peppers, broccoli, and carrots to the skillet.

Step 6: Stir-fry vegetables until crisp-tender.

Step 7: Add the cooked turkey back to the skillet and toss with the vegetables.

Step 8: Serve the teriyaki turkey and vegetable stir-fry over cooked rice or noodles. Enjoy!

Helpful Tips:
1. Marinate the turkey slices in teriyaki sauce for at least 30 minutes to enhance flavor.

2. Use a wok or large skillet to cook the stir-fry ingredients, as it allows for even cooking and quick preparation.

3. Cook the turkey slices first until they are slightly browned and cooked through before adding the vegetables.

4. Add a variety of colorful vegetables like bell peppers, broccoli, and carrots for a nutritious and visually appealing dish.

5. Keep the heat high and continually stir the ingredients to ensure they cook evenly and quickly.

6. Garnish with sesame seeds and green onions for added flavor and texture.

Greek yogurt and berry parfait

Ingredients:

- 2 cups Greek yogurt
- 1 cup mixed berries
- 4 tbsp honey
- 1/2 cup granola

Equipment:

1. Mixing bowl
2. Whisk
3. Measuring cups
4. Wooden spoon
5. Spatula

Methods:

Step 1: Gather your ingredients, including Greek yogurt, mixed berries, granola, and honey.

Step 2: In a glass or bowl, layer Greek yogurt at the bottom.

Step 3: Add a layer of mixed berries on top of the yogurt.

Step 4: Sprinkle granola over the berries.

Step 5: Drizzle honey over the granola.

Step 6: Repeat the layers until the glass is full, finishing with a final layer of yogurt on top.

Step 7: Garnish with extra berries and a final drizzle of honey if desired.

Step 8: Enjoy your delicious and healthy Greek yogurt and berry parfait!

Helpful Tips:

1. Start by layering Greek yogurt at the bottom of your serving dish.

2. Add a layer of mixed berries, such as strawberries, blueberries, and raspberries.

3. Drizzle honey or maple syrup over the berries for added sweetness.

4. Repeat the layers until you reach the top of the dish.

5. Top with a sprinkle of granola for added crunch.

6. Serve immediately or chill in the fridge for a few hours before serving.

7. Customize with additional toppings such as chopped nuts or seeds.
8. Enjoy as a healthy breakfast or a refreshing snack!

Turkey and vegetable meatballs in marinara sauce

Ingredients:
- 1 lb ground turkey
- 1/2 cup breadcrumbs
- 1/4 cup grated parmesan
- 1/4 cup chopped onion
- 1/4 cup chopped bell pepper
- 1/4 cup chopped zucchini
- 1 can marinara sauce

Equipment:
1. Mixing bowls
2. Wooden spoon
3. Knife
4. Skillet
5. Baking dish

Methods:
Step 1: Preheat the oven to 375°F and line a baking sheet with parchment paper.

Step 2: In a large bowl, combine ground turkey, minced onion, minced garlic, grated zucchini, breadcrumbs, Parmesan cheese, egg, and Italian seasoning.

Step 3: Mix all ingredients until well combined and form into meatballs.

Step 4: Place meatballs on the prepared baking sheet and bake for 20-25 minutes, or until cooked through.

Step 5: In a large skillet, heat marinara sauce over medium heat.

Step 6: Add the cooked meatballs to the marinara sauce and simmer for 10 minutes.

Step 7: Serve the turkey and vegetable meatballs over pasta or with crusty bread. Enjoy!

Helpful Tips:

THE LOW-FAT LIFESTYLE: TIPS AND RECIPES FOR A HEALTHIER HEART

1. Use lean ground turkey for healthier meatballs.

2. Add finely chopped vegetables like bell peppers, carrots, and zucchini to increase veggie intake.

3. Season the meatballs with garlic, onion powder, Italian herbs, and a pinch of red pepper flakes for extra flavor.

4. Preheat the oven before baking the meatballs to ensure they cook evenly.

5. Simmer the marinara sauce on low heat to let the flavors meld together.

6. Serve the meatballs over whole wheat spaghetti or zucchini noodles for a balanced meal.

7. Garnish with fresh basil or parsley before serving for a pop of color and freshness.

Asian-inspired shrimp lettuce wraps

Ingredients:
- 1 lb shrimp
- 1 head of lettuce
- 1/4 cup soy sauce
- 2 cloves garlic
- 1 tbsp sesame oil
- 1 tsp ginger
- 1/2 cup sliced green onions

Equipment:
1. Knife
2. Cutting board
3. Mixing bowl
4. Skillet
5. Tongs

Methods:
Step 1: Marinate shrimp in a mixture of soy sauce, garlic, ginger, and sesame oil for 30 minutes.

Step 2: Heat a pan over medium-high heat and cook shrimp until pink and cooked through.

Step 3: Remove shrimp from pan and chop into small pieces.

Step 4: In the same pan, sauté water chestnuts, bell peppers, and mushrooms until tender.

Step 5: Add the chopped shrimp back to the pan and cook for an additional 2 minutes.

Step 6: Fill lettuce leaves with the shrimp mixture and top with chopped cilantro and peanuts.

Step 7: Serve with a side of hoisin sauce for dipping. Enjoy!

Helpful Tips:
1. Marinate shrimp in soy sauce, garlic, ginger, and sesame oil for at least 30 minutes.

2. Heat a skillet over medium-high heat and cook shrimp until pink and cooked through, about 2-3 minutes per side.

3. Fill lettuce leaves with cooked shrimp, shredded carrots, cucumbers, and fresh herbs like cilantro and mint.

4. Top with a drizzle of hoisin or sweet chili sauce for added flavor.

5. Garnish with crushed peanuts or sesame seeds for a crunchy texture.

6. Serve immediately and enjoy the fresh and savory flavors of these Asian-inspired shrimp lettuce wraps.

Lentil and vegetable curry with jasmine rice

Ingredients:
- 1 cup dried lentils
- 1 onion, chopped
- 2 carrots, diced
- 1 can diced tomatoes
- 1 tsp curry powder
- 1 cup jasmine rice

Equipment:
1. Pot
2. Pan
3. Spoon
4. Knife
5. Cutting board

Methods:
Step 1: Rinse 1 cup of lentils and soak in water for 30 minutes.

Step 2: In a large pot, heat oil and sauté 1 diced onion until translucent.

Step 3: Add 2 cloves of minced garlic, 1 tsp of minced ginger, and 1 diced carrot. Cook for 2 minutes.

Step 4: Stir in 1 tbsp of curry powder, 1 tsp of cumin, and 1/2 tsp of turmeric.

Step 5: Add lentils, 1 can of diced tomatoes, and 2 cups of vegetable broth. Bring to a boil, then simmer for 20 minutes.

Step 6: Season with salt and pepper. Serve over jasmine rice. Enjoy!

Helpful Tips:
1. Start by rinsing the lentils and soaking them in water for at least 30 minutes before cooking.

2. Use a mix of your favorite vegetables such as bell peppers, carrots, and spinach for added flavor and nutrition.

3. Sautee onions, garlic, and ginger in a large pot with oil before adding in your lentils and vegetables.

4. Add in your choice of curry powder, turmeric, cumin, and coriander for a flavorful spice blend.

5. Let the curry simmer on low for at least 30 minutes to allow the flavors to meld together.

6. Serve over fluffy jasmine rice for a complete and satisfying meal.

Chicken and vegetable skewers with tzatziki sauce

Ingredients:
- 1 lb chicken breast, cut into cubes
- 1 red bell pepper, cut into chunks
- 1 zucchini, sliced
- 1 onion, cut into wedges
- 1/4 cup olive oil
- 2 cloves garlic, minced
- 1/2 tsp dried oregano
- 1/2 cup Greek yogurt
- 1/2 cucumber, grated
- 1 tbsp lemon juice
- Salt and pepper, to taste

Equipment:
1. Skewers
2. Grilling pan
3. Mixing bowl
4. Whisk
5. Cutting board
6. Knife

Methods:
Step 1: Marinate chicken cubes in a mixture of olive oil, lemon juice, garlic, salt, and pepper for at least 30 minutes.

Step 2: Thread marinated chicken onto skewers, alternating with cherry tomatoes, bell peppers, and onions.

Step 3: Preheat the grill to medium-high heat.

Step 4: Grill skewers for 10-12 minutes, turning occasionally, until chicken is cooked through and vegetables are slightly charred.

Step 5: Meanwhile, prepare the tzatziki sauce by combining Greek yogurt, cucumber, garlic, lemon juice, and dill in a bowl.

Step 6: Serve the chicken and vegetable skewers with the tzatziki sauce on the side. Enjoy!

Helpful Tips:

1. Marinate the chicken before skewering to enhance flavor.

2. Use a variety of colorful vegetables for an appealing presentation.

3. Soak wooden skewers in water for at least 30 minutes to prevent burning.

4. Preheat the grill or grill pan on high heat for a nice sear.

5. Rotate skewers occasionally for even cooking.

6. Make the tzatziki sauce ahead of time for the flavors to meld.

7. Serve skewers with a side of rice or pita bread for a complete meal.

8. Garnish with fresh herbs like parsley or dill for a pop of color.

Grilled chicken breast

Ingredients:
- 4 chicken breasts
- 1/4 cup olive oil
- 2 tbsp lemon juice
- 2 cloves garlic
- Salt and pepper to taste
(122 characters)

Equipment:
1. Knife
2. Cutting board
3. Grill pan
4. Tongs
5. Meat thermometer

Methods:
Step 1: Preheat the grill to medium-high heat.

Step 2: Season chicken breasts with salt, pepper, and any desired spices.

Step 3: Place chicken breasts on the hot grill and cook for 6-7 minutes per side.

Step 4: Use a meat thermometer to ensure the internal temperature reaches 165°F.

Step 5: Remove chicken from the grill and let it rest for a few minutes.

Step 6: Slice the chicken and serve hot with your favorite sides or on top of a salad.

Step 7: Enjoy your delicious grilled chicken breast!

Helpful Tips:
1. Marinate the chicken breast in a mixture of olive oil, lemon juice, garlic, and herbs for at least 30 minutes.

2. Preheat the grill to medium-high heat before placing the chicken on the grates.

3. Cook the chicken breast for about 6-8 minutes per side, or until the internal temperature reaches 165°F.

4. Avoid overcooking the chicken to prevent it from becoming tough and dry.

5. Let the chicken rest for a few minutes before slicing and serving to allow the juices to redistribute.

6. Serve the grilled chicken breast with your favorite sides and enjoy!

Steamed salmon

Ingredients:
- 4 salmon fillets
- 1 lemon, sliced
- 4 sprigs of fresh dill
- Salt and pepper

Equipment:
1. Knife
2. Cutting board
3. Pot
4. Pan
5. Spatula

Methods:
Step 1: Season the salmon fillets with salt and pepper.

Step 2: Place a steamer basket in a large pot filled with water, making sure the water does not touch the basket.

Step 3: Bring the water to a simmer over medium heat.

Step 4: Place the seasoned salmon fillets in the steamer basket.

Step 5: Cover the pot with a lid and steam the salmon for about 6-8 minutes, or until it is cooked through and flakes easily with a fork.

Step 6: Remove the pot from heat and carefully take out the steamed salmon.

Step 7: Serve the salmon with your favorite side dishes and enjoy!

Helpful Tips:
1. Use high-quality salmon fillets for best results.

2. Season the salmon with salt, pepper, and your favorite herbs or spices.

3. Place the salmon on a steaming rack or in a steamer basket.

4. Steam the salmon for about 10-15 minutes or until it flakes easily with a fork.

5. Add fresh lemon juice or a drizzle of olive oil before serving.

6. Garnish with chopped fresh herbs or citrus zest for a pop of flavor.

7. Serve with steamed vegetables or rice for a complete meal.

Baked tilapia

Ingredients:
- 4 tilapia fillets
- 1 lemon
- 2 tablespoons olive oil
- Salt and pepper to taste

Equipment:
1. Baking sheet
2. Oven mitts
3. Baking dish
4. Measuring cups
5. Kitchen thermometer

Methods:
Step 1: Preheat the oven to 400°F (200°C) and lightly grease a baking dish.

Step 2: Rinse the tilapia fillets under cold water and pat them dry with paper towels.

Step 3: Place the fillets in the prepared baking dish and season with salt and pepper.

Step 4: In a small bowl, mix together melted butter, lemon juice, and minced garlic.

Step 5: Pour the butter mixture over the tilapia fillets.

Step 6: Bake in the preheated oven for 15-20 minutes, or until the fish is opaque and flakes easily with a fork.

Step 7: Serve hot and enjoy your delicious baked tilapia!

Helpful Tips:
1. Preheat your oven to 400°F and line a baking sheet with parchment paper.

2. Season the tilapia fillets with salt, pepper, and any desired herbs and spices.

3. Place the seasoned fillets on the prepared baking sheet.

4. Drizzle olive oil or melted butter over the fish to keep it moist.

5. Bake for about 15-20 minutes or until the fish flakes easily with a fork.

6. Serve the baked tilapia with lemon wedges for a burst of freshness.

7. Don't overcook the tilapia as it can become dry and rubbery.

8. Experiment with different toppings like breadcrumbs, Parmesan cheese, or a squeeze of fresh lime juice.

Turkey meatballs

Ingredients:
- 1 lb ground turkey
- 1/2 cup breadcrumbs
- 1/4 cup grated Parmesan
- 1/4 cup chopped parsley
- 1 egg, beaten
- 1 clove garlic, minced
- Salt and pepper to taste

Equipment:
1. Mixing bowl
2. Wooden spoon
3. Baking sheet
4. Skillet
5. Measuring cups
6. Tongs

Methods:
Step 1: Preheat the oven to 400°F and line a baking sheet with parchment paper.

Step 2: In a large mixing bowl, combine ground turkey, breadcrumbs, finely chopped onion, minced garlic, beaten egg, chopped parsley, salt, pepper, and any additional seasonings of your choice.

Step 3: Mix the ingredients together until well combined but do not overmix.

Step 4: Roll the mixture into small meatballs, about 1 inch in diameter, and place them on the prepared baking sheet.

Step 5: Bake the meatballs in the preheated oven for 20-25 minutes or until cooked through.

Step 6: Serve the turkey meatballs hot with your favorite sauce or pasta. Enjoy!

Helpful Tips:

1. Mix ground turkey with breadcrumbs, egg, onion, garlic, and herbs for flavorful meatballs.

2. Use a combination of white and dark meat for a juicy texture.

3. Roll meatballs into evenly sized portions for even cooking.

4. Brown meatballs in a skillet before simmering in marinara sauce for added flavor.

5. Add grated parmesan or pecorino cheese to the meatball mixture for a cheesy twist.

6. Bake meatballs in the oven for a healthier option instead of frying.

7. Use a meat thermometer to ensure meatballs are cooked through to 165°F.

Vegetable stir-fry

Ingredients:

- 2 cups mixed vegetables
- 1/4 cup soy sauce
- 2 cloves garlic, minced
- 1 tbsp vegetable oil

Equipment:

1. Wok
2. Spatula
3. Chef's knife
4. Cutting board
5. Cooking oil
6. Serving bowl

Methods:

Step 1: Heat a skillet or wok over high heat.

Step 2: Add 1 tablespoon of oil and swirl to coat the pan.

Step 3: Add chopped vegetables such as bell peppers, carrots, broccoli, and snap peas.

Step 4: Stir constantly for 3-5 minutes, or until vegetables are tender-crisp.

Step 5: In a small bowl, mix together soy sauce, garlic, ginger, and a pinch of sugar.

Step 6: Pour the sauce over the vegetables and toss to coat.

Step 7: Cook for another 1-2 minutes, or until the sauce thickens slightly.

Step 8: Serve hot over rice or noodles. Enjoy your vegetable stir-fry!

Helpful Tips:

1. Make sure to cut all your vegetables into uniform sizes to ensure even cooking.

2. Preheat your skillet or wok over medium-high heat before adding oil to prevent sticking.

3. Add vegetables that take longer to cook (such as carrots or broccoli) first, then add quicker-cooking vegetables (like bell peppers or snap peas) later.

4. Stir frequently to prevent burning and ensure vegetables are evenly cooked.

5. For added flavor, consider adding minced garlic, ginger, or soy sauce to your stir-fry.

6. Serve over rice or noodles for a complete meal.

Low-fat turkey chili

Ingredients:
- 1 lb lean ground turkey
- 1 can low-sodium kidney beans
- 1 can low-sodium diced tomatoes
- 1 onion, chopped

Equipment:
1. Pot
2. Wooden spoon
3. Knife
4. Cutting board
5. Ladle

Methods:
Step 1: Heat 1 tablespoon of olive oil in a large pot over medium heat

Step 2: Add 1 diced onion and 2 minced garlic cloves, sauté until softened

Step 3: Stir in 1 pound of lean ground turkey, cook until browned

Step 4: Add 1 diced bell pepper, 1 diced zucchini, and 1 cup of frozen corn

Step 5: Mix in 2 cans of diced tomatoes, 1 can of low-sodium kidney beans, and 2 tablespoons of chili powder

Step 6: Bring to a simmer and let cook for 30 minutes

Step 7: Serve hot with optional toppings like low-fat cheese and Greek yogurt

Helpful Tips:
1. Use lean ground turkey instead of higher-fat meats like beef.

2. Add plenty of veggies like bell peppers, onions, and tomatoes for extra flavor and nutrients.

3. Use low-sodium chicken or vegetable broth instead of high-fat beef broth.

4. Opt for kidney beans or black beans for added protein and fiber.

5. Season with spices like chili powder, cumin, and paprika for a flavorful kick without added fat.

6. Top with low-fat Greek yogurt or a sprinkle of reduced-fat cheese instead of full-fat sour cream.

7. Serve with a side of whole grain bread or brown rice for a complete, balanced meal.

Black bean soup

Ingredients:
- 2 cans black beans
- 1 onion, chopped
- 2 cloves garlic, minced
- 1 tsp cumin
- 4 cups vegetable broth
- Salt and pepper to taste

Equipment:
1. Pot
2. Ladle
3. Immersion blender
4. Cutting board
5. Knife

Methods:
Step 1: Soak 1 pound of black beans in water overnight.

Step 2: Drain the soaked beans and rinse under cold water.

Step 3: In a large pot, sauté diced onions, carrots, and celery in olive oil until tender.

Step 4: Add the soaked beans, chicken or vegetable broth, and seasonings (such as cumin, garlic, and bay leaf).

Step 5: Bring the soup to a boil, then reduce heat and simmer for 1-2 hours, until the beans are tender.

Step 6: Optional: use an immersion blender to partially blend the soup for a thicker consistency.

Step 7: Serve hot and enjoy with toppings like sour cream, avocado, and cilantro.

Helpful Tips:
1. Soak the black beans overnight to reduce cooking time and improve digestibility.

2. Sauté onions, garlic, and bell peppers before adding the black beans to enhance flavor.

3. Use a mixture of broth and water for a balanced flavor profile.

4. Add cumin, chili powder, and a bay leaf for a depth of flavor.

5. Blend a portion of the soup for a creamy texture, while leaving some beans whole for texture.

6. Add a splash of lime juice and a dollop of sour cream or yogurt before serving for added freshness.

Grilled shrimp skewers

Ingredients:
- 1 pound of large shrimp
- 1/4 cup of olive oil
- 2 cloves of garlic, minced
- 1 tablespoon of lemon juice
- Salt and pepper to taste
- Wooden skewers

Equipment:
1. Grill
2. Skewers
3. Tongs
4. Knife
5. Cutting board

Methods:
Step 1: Soak wooden skewers in water for at least 30 minutes to prevent burning.

Step 2: Preheat grill to medium-high heat.

Step 3: Thread peeled and deveined shrimp onto skewers, leaving space between each shrimp.

Step 4: Brush shrimp with olive oil and season with salt, pepper, and any desired spices or herbs.

Step 5: Place the skewers on the grill and cook for 2-3 minutes per side, or until shrimp is opaque and slightly charred.

Step 6: Remove skewers from grill and let rest for a few minutes before serving.

Step 7: Enjoy your delicious grilled shrimp skewers!

Helpful Tips:
1. Soak skewers in water for at least 30 minutes before threading the shrimp to prevent them from burning on the grill.

2. Marinate shrimp in a mixture of olive oil, minced garlic, lemon juice, and your favorite herbs and spices for at least 30 minutes before grilling for added flavor.

3. Preheat the grill to medium-high heat before cooking the skewers to ensure they cook evenly and quickly.

4. Cook shrimp skewers for about 2-3 minutes per side or until they turn pink and opaque.

5. Serve shrimp skewers with a side of grilled vegetables or a fresh salad for a well-rounded meal.

Tofu stir-fry

Ingredients:
- 400g tofu
- 2 tablespoons soy sauce
- 1 tablespoon sesame oil
- 1 bell pepper
- 1 onion
- 2 cloves garlic
- 1 teaspoon ginger
- 1 tablespoon vegetable oil

Equipment:
1. Wok
2. Spatula
3. Cooking oil
4. Knife
5. Cutting board

Methods:
Step 1: Press tofu to remove excess water and cut into cubes.

Step 2: Heat oil in a large skillet or wok over medium-high heat.

Step 3: Add tofu cubes and cook until golden brown on all sides.

Step 4: Remove tofu from skillet and set aside.

Step 5: In the same skillet, add sliced vegetables (such as bell peppers, broccoli, and carrots) and stir-fry until slightly tender.

Step 6: Add tofu back into the skillet with vegetables.

Step 7: Pour in a mixture of soy sauce, sesame oil, and ginger.

Step 8: Stir-fry for a few more minutes until everything is well combined.

Step 9: Serve hot over rice or noodles. Enjoy!

Helpful Tips:
1. Press the tofu for at least 30 minutes to remove excess moisture and improve the texture.

2. Cut the tofu into cubes or strips for even cooking and easy serving.

3. Marinate the tofu in soy sauce, ginger, and garlic for added flavor before stir-frying.

4. Use a high heat oil like sesame or peanut oil for a delicious nutty flavor.

5. Add plenty of colorful vegetables like bell peppers, broccoli, and snow peas for a nutritious and visually appealing stir-fry.

6. Stir-fry quickly to prevent the tofu from becoming too mushy.

Egg white omelette

Ingredients:
- 8 egg whites
- 1/4 cup diced onions
- 1/4 cup diced bell peppers
- 1/4 cup diced tomatoes

Equipment:
1. Frying pan
2. Whisk
3. Spatula
4. Mixing bowl
5. Knife

Methods:
Step 1: Crack open 4-5 eggs and separate the whites from the yolks.

Step 2: Whisk the egg whites until they are frothy and slightly stiff.

Step 3: Heat a non-stick skillet over medium heat and add a small amount of oil or cooking spray.

Step 4: Pour the whisked egg whites into the skillet and spread them out evenly.

Step 5: Cook the egg whites for 2-3 minutes, or until they begin to set.

Step 6: Add desired toppings such as vegetables, cheese, or herbs to one half of the omelette.

Step 7: Fold the other half of the omelette over the toppings and cook for an additional 1-2 minutes.

Step 8: Slide the omelette onto a plate and serve hot. Enjoy!

Helpful Tips:
1. Separate the egg whites carefully to avoid getting any yolk, as even a small amount can prevent the whites from properly fluffing up.

2. Beat the egg whites until stiff peaks form to ensure a light and fluffy omelette.

3. Cook the omelette on low heat to prevent the egg whites from turning rubbery or browning too quickly.

4. Add your desired fillings just before folding the omelette to avoid overcooking the delicate egg whites.

5. Consider adding a pinch of salt to enhance the flavor of the egg whites, as they can be bland on their own.

Spinach salad with grilled chicken

Ingredients:
- 2 chicken breasts
- 4 cups fresh spinach
- 1 cup cherry tomatoes
- 1/2 cup feta cheese
- 1/4 cup balsamic vinaigrette

Equipment:
1. Knife
2. Cutting board
3. Grill pan
4. Tongs
5. Salad bowl
6. Plate

Methods:
Step 1: Marinate the chicken with olive oil, lemon juice, salt, pepper, and garlic for at least 30 minutes.

Step 2: Preheat a grill or grill pan over medium heat.

Step 3: Cook the marinated chicken on the grill for about 6-8 minutes per side or until fully cooked.

Step 4: Let the chicken rest for a few minutes before slicing it.

Step 5: In a large bowl, mix together spinach, cherry tomatoes, red onion, and any other desired salad toppings.

Step 6: Drizzle with balsamic vinaigrette and toss to combine.

Step 7: Top the salad with the sliced grilled chicken and serve.

Helpful Tips:
1. Start by marinating the chicken in olive oil, lemon juice, salt, pepper, and garlic for at least 30 minutes before grilling.

2. Make a simple dressing by mixing olive oil, balsamic vinegar, Dijon mustard, honey, salt, and pepper in a small bowl.

3. Toss fresh spinach leaves with cherry tomatoes, sliced cucumber, red onion, and crumbled feta cheese in a large salad bowl.

4. Grill the marinated chicken until it reaches an internal temperature of 165°F, then slice it thinly.

5. Drizzle the dressing over the salad and top with the grilled chicken slices for a delicious and nutritious meal.

Lentil soup

Ingredients:
- 1 cup red lentils
- 1 onion, diced
- 2 carrots, chopped
- 2 celery stalks, diced
- 4 cups vegetable broth
- 1 tsp cumin
- 1/2 tsp turmeric
- 1/4 tsp cayenne pepper

Equipment:
1. Pot
2. Ladle
3. Cutting board
4. Knife
5. Wooden spoon

Methods:
Step 1: Rinse 1 cup of lentils under cold water and set aside.

Step 2: In a large pot, heat 1 tablespoon of olive oil over medium heat.

Step 3: Add 1 diced onion, 2 chopped carrots, and 2 minced cloves of garlic to the pot. Cook until softened, about 5 minutes.

Step 4: Pour in 4 cups of vegetable broth and the rinsed lentils.

Step 5: Season with salt, pepper, and any desired herbs or spices.

Step 6: Bring the soup to a boil, then reduce heat and let simmer for 20-25 minutes, or until lentils are tender.

Step 7: Serve hot and enjoy!

Helpful Tips:
1. Start by rinsing the lentils under cold water to remove any dirt or debris.
2. Sauté onions, garlic, and carrots in olive oil for added flavor.
3. Use vegetable broth instead of water for a richer taste.
4. Add some diced tomatoes for depth and a touch of acidity.

5. Season with salt, pepper, and herbs like thyme or bay leaves.

6. Consider adding chopped kale or spinach for extra nutrition.

7. Let the soup simmer on low heat for at least 30 minutes to allow flavors to meld.

8. Serve with a squeeze of lemon juice or a dollop of yogurt for a tangy finish. Enjoy!

Grilled vegetable sandwich

Ingredients:
- 1 zucchini, sliced
- 1 red bell pepper, sliced
- 1 yellow bell pepper, sliced
- 1 red onion, sliced
- 1/4 cup olive oil
- Salt and pepper to taste
- 8 slices of bread
- 4 slices of provolone cheese

Equipment:
1. Knife
2. Cutting board
3. Skillet
4. Spatula
5. Grill pan
6. Toaster

Methods:
Step 1: Preheat the grill to medium-high heat.

Step 2: Drizzle olive oil over a selection of sliced vegetables such as zucchini, eggplant, bell peppers, and onions.

Step 3: Season the vegetables with salt, pepper, and any desired herbs or spices.

Step 4: Place the vegetables on the grill and cook for about 3-4 minutes per side, or until they are tender and have grill marks.

Step 5: Spread hummus or pesto on two slices of bread.

Step 6: Layer the grilled vegetables on one slice of bread and top with the other slice.

Step 7: Grill the sandwich for a few minutes on each side until the bread is toasted and the filling is heated through.

Step 8: Serve hot and enjoy your delicious grilled vegetable sandwich!

Helpful Tips:

1. Preheat your grill pan or outdoor grill to medium heat.

2. Slice your favorite vegetables such as bell peppers, zucchini, eggplant, and mushrooms.

3. Drizzle the veggies with olive oil and season with salt, pepper, and any desired herbs or seasonings.

4. Grill the veggies until they are tender and have grill marks, about 3-5 minutes per side.

5. Toast your bread or bun on the grill until lightly charred.

6. Assemble your sandwich with the grilled vegetables, some fresh greens, and a spread such as pesto or hummus.

7. Enjoy your delicious and healthy grilled vegetable sandwich!

Baked chicken tenders

Ingredients:
- 1 lb chicken breast tenders
- 1/2 cup bread crumbs
- 1/4 cup grated Parmesan
- 1 tsp garlic powder
- Salt and pepper to taste

Equipment:
1. Baking sheet
2. Tongs
3. Oven
4. Mixing bowl
5. Whisk

Methods:
Step 1: Preheat the oven to 400°F.

Step 2: In a bowl, mix together breadcrumbs, grated Parmesan cheese, salt, pepper, garlic powder, and paprika.

Step 3: Dip chicken tenders into beaten eggs, then coat with breadcrumb mixture.

Step 4: Place coated chicken tenders on a baking sheet lined with parchment paper.

Step 5: Drizzle chicken tenders with olive oil.

Step 6: Bake in the preheated oven for 15-20 minutes or until the chicken is cooked through and the coating is crispy.

Step 7: Serve hot with your favorite dipping sauces. Enjoy!

Helpful Tips:
1. Preheat your oven to 400°F for perfectly crispy chicken tenders.

2. Use a wire rack on a baking sheet to ensure the heat circulates evenly around the tenders.

3. Season the chicken tenders with a blend of spices like garlic powder, paprika, salt, and pepper.

4. Dip each tender in whisked eggs, then coat with breadcrumbs or crushed cornflakes for added crunch.

5. Bake for 20-25 minutes, flipping halfway through, until the outside is golden brown and the inside is cooked through.

6. Serve with your favorite dipping sauce for a delicious and satisfying meal.

Poached cod

Ingredients:
- 4 cod fillets
- 2 cups of fish stock
- 1 lemon, sliced
- 4 sprigs of thyme

Equipment:
1. Saucepan
2. Slotted spoon
3. Tongs
4. Fish spatula
5. Thermometer
6. Plate

Methods:
Step 1: Bring a large pot of water to a gentle simmer.

Step 2: Add in aromatics such as herbs, garlic, and lemon slices to flavor the poaching liquid.

Step 3: Season the cod fillets with salt and pepper.

Step 4: Carefully lower the cod fillets into the simmering water.

Step 5: Poach the cod for 7-10 minutes, or until the fish is opaque and flakes easily with a fork.

Step 6: Remove the cod from the water using a slotted spoon.

Step 7: Serve the poached cod with a drizzle of olive oil, a squeeze of lemon, and fresh herbs. Enjoy your delicious and healthy meal!

Helpful Tips:
1. Use a deep skillet or wide saucepan to poach the cod to ensure the fish is fully submerged in the poaching liquid.

2. Season the poaching liquid with aromatics like garlic, herbs, and bay leaves to infuse flavor into the cod.

3. Bring the poaching liquid to a gentle simmer, not a rapid boil, to prevent the cod from falling apart.

4. Check the internal temperature of the cod with a thermometer to ensure it reaches 140°F (60°C) for safe consumption.

5. Serve the poached cod with a drizzle of olive oil, a squeeze of lemon, and fresh herbs for a simple and delicious dish.

Mushroom and barley soup

Ingredients:

- 1 cup pearl barley
- 8 cups vegetable broth
- 1 onion, diced
- 2 cloves garlic, minced
- 2 cups sliced mushrooms
- Salt and pepper to taste

Equipment:

1. Pot
2. Ladle
3. Cutting board
4. Knife
5. Wooden spoon

Methods:

Step 1: In a large pot, heat olive oil over medium heat.

Step 2: Add chopped onions and garlic, sauté until soft.

Step 3: Add sliced mushrooms and cook until they release their juices.

Step 4: Stir in vegetable broth, diced carrots, chopped celery, and barley.

Step 5: Season with salt, pepper, and herbs of your choice.

Step 6: Bring the soup to a boil, then reduce heat and simmer for 45 minutes.

Step 7: Check barley for tenderness, adjust seasoning if needed.

Step 8: Serve hot, garnished with fresh parsley. Enjoy your hearty mushroom and barley soup!

Helpful Tips:

1. Start by sautéing diced onions, carrots, and celery in olive oil to bring out their flavors.

2. Add sliced mushrooms and cook until they release their juices and become golden brown.

3. Stir in barley and a combination of vegetable broth and water for a hearty base.

4. Season with dried thyme, salt, and pepper for a comforting and aromatic soup.

5. Let the soup simmer on low heat until the barley is fully cooked and the flavors have melded together.

6. Serve hot with a sprinkle of fresh parsley for a delicious and satisfying meal.

Grilled portobello mushrooms

Ingredients:

- 4 large portobello mushrooms
- 2 tablespoons olive oil
- 1 teaspoon balsamic vinegar
- Salt and pepper to taste

Equipment:

1. Grill pan
2. Wooden spatula
3. Tongs
4. Basting brush
5. Aluminum foil
6. Kitchen knife

Methods:

Step 1: Preheat the grill to medium-high heat.

Step 2: Clean the portobello mushrooms, removing stems and any dirt.

Step 3: Brush mushrooms with olive oil and season with salt and pepper.

Step 4: Place mushrooms on grill, gill side down, and cook for 5-7 minutes.

Step 5: Flip mushrooms and cook for an additional 5-7 minutes, or until tender.

Step 6: Optional - add garlic, herbs, or balsamic vinegar for extra flavor.

Step 7: Remove mushrooms from grill and serve immediately.

Step 8: Enjoy your delicious grilled portobello mushrooms!

Helpful Tips:

1. Preheat your grill to medium-high heat.

2. Clean your Portobello mushrooms by wiping them with a damp paper towel.

3. Remove the stems from the mushrooms and brush both sides with olive oil.

4. Season with salt, pepper, and your favorite herbs or spices.

5. Grill the mushrooms for about 5-7 minutes per side, or until they are tender.

6. Top them with cheese or a balsamic glaze for extra flavor.

7. Serve the grilled Portobello mushrooms as a side dish or on a burger bun for a meatless meal.

Lemon herb baked fish

Ingredients:
- 4 fillets of white fish
- 1 lemon
- 2 tbsp olive oil
- 1 tsp dried herbs
- Salt and pepper to taste

Equipment:
1. Baking dish
2. Mixing bowl
3. Knife
4. Cutting board
5. Oven
6. Aluminum foil

Methods:
Step 1: Preheat the oven to 400°F.

Step 2: Pat dry the fish fillets with paper towels.

Step 3: In a small bowl, mix together chopped herbs (such as dill, parsley, and thyme), minced garlic, lemon zest, and olive oil.

Step 4: Season the fish fillets with salt and pepper, then place them on a baking dish.

Step 5: Spread the herb mixture evenly on top of the fish.

Step 6: Squeeze fresh lemon juice over the fish.

Step 7: Bake in the oven for about 15-20 minutes, or until the fish is cooked through and flakes easily with a fork.

Step 8: Serve hot and enjoy!

Helpful Tips:
1. Preheat your oven to 375°F.

2. Season the fish with salt, pepper, and your choice of herbs like dill, parsley, or thyme.

3. Squeeze fresh lemon juice over the fish for extra flavor.

4. Place the fish in a baking dish and drizzle with olive oil.

5. Cover the dish with foil and bake for 15-20 minutes until the fish is cooked through and flakes easily with a fork.

6. Garnish with fresh herbs and lemon slices before serving.

7. Serve with steamed vegetables or a light salad for a healthy meal.

8. Enjoy the delicious and nutritious lemon herb baked fish!

Spaghetti squash with marinara sauce

Ingredients:

- 1 medium spaghetti squash
- 2 cups marinara sauce
- 1/2 tsp salt
- 1/4 tsp black pepper

Equipment:

1. Pot
2. Strainer
3. Pan
4. Spoon
5. Knife

Methods:

Step 1: Preheat the oven to 375°F.

Step 2: Cut the spaghetti squash in half lengthwise and scoop out the seeds.

Step 3: Place the squash halves cut side down on a baking sheet.

Step 4: Roast in the oven for 40-50 minutes, or until the squash is tender.

Step 5: While the squash is cooking, heat marinara sauce on the stove.

Step 6: Use a fork to scrape out the squash flesh, creating "spaghetti" strands.

Step 7: Serve the spaghetti squash topped with marinara sauce and your choice of toppings, such as Parmesan cheese or fresh herbs.

Step 8: Enjoy your delicious and healthy meal!

Helpful Tips:

1. Preheat oven to 400°F.

2. Cut spaghetti squash in half lengthwise and scoop out seeds.

3. Place squash cut-side down on a baking sheet and bake for 45-50 minutes, or until tender.

4. Meanwhile, heat marinara sauce in a saucepan over low heat.

5. Once squash is cooked, use a fork to separate strands.

6. Serve squash topped with marinara sauce and grated Parmesan cheese, if desired.

7. Feel free to add cooked ground beef or turkey to the marinara sauce for added protein.

8. Enjoy your delicious and healthy spaghetti squash with marinara sauce!

Eggplant and zucchini bake

Ingredients:
- 1 eggplant, sliced
- 1 zucchini, sliced
- 1 cup marinara sauce
- 1 cup shredded mozzarella

Equipment:
1. Baking dish
2. Knife
3. Cutting Board
4. Mixing bowl
5. Oven
6. Spoon

Methods:
Step 1: Preheat the oven to 375°F.

Step 2: Wash and slice 1 eggplant and 2 zucchinis into thin rounds.

Step 3: Spread a layer of marinara sauce on the bottom of a baking dish.

Step 4: Arrange a layer of eggplant slices on top of the marinara sauce.

Step 5: Sprinkle with salt, pepper, and dried herbs.

Step 6: Add a layer of zucchini slices on top of the eggplant.

Step 7: Repeat layers until all the vegetables are used.

Step 8: Top with shredded mozzarella cheese.

Step 9: Cover with foil and bake for 30 minutes.

Step 10: Remove foil and bake for an additional 10 minutes until cheese is bubbly and golden.

Step 11: Let it cool before serving. Enjoy your delicious eggplant and zucchini bake!

Helpful Tips:
1. Preheat your oven to 375°F and grease a baking dish.
2. Slice the eggplant and zucchini into equal-sized rounds.

3. Layer the eggplant and zucchini rounds in the baking dish, alternating between the two.

4. Season the vegetables with salt, pepper, and herbs of your choice.

5. Pour a mixture of olive oil and marinara sauce over the layered vegetables.

6. Top with a generous amount of grated Parmesan cheese.

7. Cover the dish with foil and bake for 45 minutes, then remove the foil and bake for an additional 15 minutes.

8. Let the bake cool for a few minutes before serving. Enjoy! (Note: Total words 96)

Roasted vegetable salad

Ingredients:

- 2 bell peppers, sliced
- 1 zucchini, sliced
- 1 red onion, diced
- 1 cup cherry tomatoes
- 2 tbsp olive oil
- Salt and pepper to taste

Equipment:

1. Knife
2. Cutting board
3. Mixing bowl
4. Baking sheet
5. Tongs

Methods:

Step 1: Preheat the oven to 400°F.

Step 2: Wash and chop your choice of vegetables such as bell peppers, zucchini, carrots, and red onions.

Step 3: Toss the vegetables with olive oil, salt, pepper, and any desired herbs or seasonings.

Step 4: Spread the vegetables out in a single layer on a baking sheet.

Step 5: Roast the vegetables in the preheated oven for 25-30 minutes, or until they are tender and slightly browned.

Step 6: Remove the vegetables from the oven and let them cool slightly.

Step 7: Arrange the roasted vegetables on a serving platter and drizzle with balsamic vinegar or a vinaigrette dressing.

Step 8: Serve the roasted vegetable salad warm or at room temperature. Enjoy!

Helpful Tips:

1. Preheat your oven to 400°F to ensure even cooking.

2. Cut your vegetables into evenly-sized pieces to ensure they cook at the same rate.

3. Toss the vegetables in olive oil, salt, pepper, and any desired seasonings before roasting.

4. Spread the vegetables in a single layer on a baking sheet to prevent them from steaming instead of roasting.

5. Roast the vegetables for about 20-30 minutes, or until they are tender and slightly caramelized.

6. Let the vegetables cool slightly before adding them to your salad to prevent wilting your greens.

7. Customize your salad with additional toppings like nuts, seeds, or cheese for extra flavor and texture.

Milton Keynes UK
Ingram Content Group UK Ltd.
UKHW022036290324
440241UK00014B/538